40 PRAYERS

FOR THE CHRISTMAS SEASON

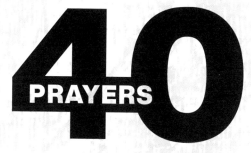

40 PRAYERS

FOR THE CHRISTMAS SEASON

Prayers for your Church or small group

DAVID CLOWES

DAVID C COOK

transforming lives together

40 PRAYERS FOR THE CHRISTMAS SEASON
Published by David C Cook
4050 Lee Vance Drive
Colorado Springs, CO 80918 U.S.A.

Integrity Music Limited, a Division of David C Cook
Brighton, East Sussex BN1 2RE, England

ISBN 978-0-8307-8231-4
eISBN 978-0-8307-8239-0

© 2020 David Clowes

The Team: Ian Matthews, Jack Campbell,
Jo Stockdale, Susan Murdock
Cover Design: Pete Barnsley

Printed in the United Kingdom
First Edition 2020

1 2 3 4 5 6 7 8 9 10

090120

CONTENTS

INTRODUCTION

Having published *500 Prayers for All Occasions* and *500 More Prayers for All Occasions* I was asked to develop a new series of books of prayer for use in small groups or in the home.

There are at least forty prayers in each of these books based around a single theme. Most of the content comes from my first two books of prayer for public worship, but has been revised and re-worked to make it appropriate for use in churches, small groups, the family situation, or for personal quiet time devotions.

My church background was firmly in the camp of extemporary prayer. I started to write my prayers down due to nervousness and on the advice of my preaching mentor who insisted on careful preparation not only of the hymns, readings, and sermon, but also of the prayers. I have long since realised the value of having a resource to be used as a flexible launch pad for my own prayer life which I could use and adapt as I wished.

I hope that is how you will approach these simple aids to prayer. They have been deliberately written in an uncomplicated style and with language that seeks to illuminate the joy of prayer. I have also tried to ensure that they are written in the language we use in our daily conversations. The aim of this is designed to make them easier to 'pray' and not simply to 'read'.

David Clowes
Stockport, April 2020

PRAYERS OF APPROACH

NOT JUST FOR CHRISTMAS

In our times of darkness, Christ comes with his light.
In our moments of loneliness, Christ comes to walk with us.
In our experiences of loss, Christ comes to share our pain.
In our times of emptiness, Christ comes to fill us.
In our experiences of brokenness, Christ comes to hold us.
In our times of delight and despair, of joy and sorrow,
of faith and of doubt,
Christ still comes—for me and for you.
No matter who we are or what we have done,
Christ comes. **Amen.**

READY FOR CHRISTMAS

Heavenly Father,
we praise you for all you have shown us in Jesus,
now we know that you are not far away.
We thank you that though we cannot see you,
you have promised that
no matter who or what we are,

no matter what we have done or failed to do,
you will be very near to each and every one of us.
As we prepare for Christmas,
help us to remember the coming of Jesus.

We praise you for the joy of his living presence in our lives.
Father, we praise you that he came into this world,
just as we did, as a helpless baby.
We thank you that his coming has left us in no doubt
about your love and mercy.
We praise you that he has opened the way to real life now
and for all eternity.
We praise you for the story of Mary and Joseph,
the shepherds and the angels,
the wise men and the star.

We praise you for the carols we sing
and the joy we share in celebrating the arrival of Jesus.
We are all the more thankful that it is not just a story
but a message of the birth of the Saviour of the world.

Forgive us, Father, if we spend so much time
preparing to enjoy ourselves
that we forget those who will have no joy this Christmas.
Forgive us that as we decorate our homes
we forget those who have no home.
Forgive us if, as we welcome the baby in the manger,
we forget he is the man on the cross.
We make our prayer in the name of Jesus,
who came and still comes. **Amen.**

CHRISTMAS EVE

Lord, we are preparing to celebrate your birthday
but we find it so easy to forget why you came.
We sing our carols and say our prayers
but when we open our presents and spend time with our
family and friends,
we find it so hard to make space for you.
We know that Christmas loses its meaning
when we forget to place you at the centre of all we say and do.
We have come today, on the eve of Christmas,
to praise you for loving us enough
to be born into our world to make us your new people.
Help us to remember that you came
to change our selfish ways
and to be the centre of our lives.
We are sorry that, even at Christmas,
we think more about what we want,
instead of what you are wanting to give.
We are sorry that, even at Christmas, we think about
ourselves and our family
and not enough about you or those who don't know you.
Forgive us and, by your love, change our hearts
and change our minds.
In Jesus' name. **Amen.**

CHRISTMAS EVE

Lord, we thank you that you have made yourself known to us
and you have done so in a way that we could understand;
that in the coming of your Son, Jesus Christ,

you have brought an end to our empty speculation
as to who you are and whether or not you love us;
that you have not only revealed yourself to us
but also that in the simplicity of Christ's coming,
you have swept away any reliance on ourselves—
our intellectual searchings or the assumption
of our personal worth.
We thank you that his being born of an earthly mother
and his entering into our world in the poverty of a stable
speaks to us of the depths to which you are
prepared to reach down
in order to lift us to the height of your throne of grace;
that his coming teaches us to be open to your coming to us
when we least expect it and in ways
we would never have dreamt possible.
We thank you that Jesus was born as a human being
and shared all our limitations of time and place;
that though he was King of Kings and Lord of Lords
he was not born into a life of privilege
but grew in knowledge of you and your purposes for him.
We thank you for all those who, like Mary,
have been prepared to say yes to you
and to your will for their lives;
for those who, like the shepherds, are so open to you
that they respond with a sense of urgency to do your will;
for those who, like Joseph, are prepared
to serve you in the background,
to remain almost unnoticed and remain faithful
at great cost to themselves.
Lord, we have come to prepare ourselves

to celebrate not only your coming
but also your living, your dying, and your rising again.
We come to celebrate the victory of your love,
a victory into which, by your Spirit,
we can enter today and every day of our lives.
Lord, we thank you, and we always will,
and we will do so in and through Christ our Lord. **Amen.**

CHRISTMAS EVE

Lord, we have come to prepare for your coming.
In the hurly-burly of our Christmas
we have left no time to meet with you.
In our crowded lives we have no space left to wait for you.
In the noise of our emptiness and our endless chatter
we have no silence left in which you can speak.
In all our activities, all our comings and goings,
we have left you out of all of our preparations,
and we are sorry.
Lord, there are times when we feel
as if we are living such empty, futile lives.
We have existence, but we have heard
that you came to give us life.
We have lost our way, but we were told that you came to
show us the way back home.
We have lost hope, but we are discovering
that you came to be our hope.
We often feel ashamed, ill-prepared, damaged, and used.
We are less than the persons you meant us to be,
but we have found that the Christ-child came

that we might begin again.
Lord, there are moments
when you break through our hardened, apathetic defences
and share your love.
Lord, we have heard the story
of your coming so many times before.
In years gone by, we have sung our carols
to celebrate your coming.
We have memories of Christmases we once enjoyed.
Lord, come again.
Enable us, by your Holy Spirit, to make those preparations
that will ensure that the Christ-child has room
and that, this year, we will truly celebrate his coming.

Amen.

THE STORY OF CHRISTMAS

Lord, we have come to praise you
as we sing our carols and listen again
to the story of the first Christmas.
We have come to remember Mary and Joseph,
the angels and the shepherds, the wise men and the star,
and the baby in the manger.
We thank you that the story of Christmas is not just a story.
We thank you that when we have opened all our presents
and eaten all the food,
when we have been to all our parties
and played all our games,
you will still be offering your love to us.
When we feel lost, in Jesus you come to find us.

When we feel alone, in Jesus
you have promised to be with us.
When we are sad, in Jesus you share our tears.
When we do not know which way to go,
in Jesus you show us the way.
When we are hurting inside, and no one seems to care,
when we are excited, and there is no one to share it,
when we are full of questions, surrounded by problems,
and no one can give us an answer,
in Jesus you show us the way.
Lord, we have come to praise and thank you for Jesus
because without him
there would be no Christmas to celebrate at all.
Help us to keep him at the centre of our Christmas,
knowing that we are at the heart of his love.
In Jesus' name. **Amen.**

WE THANK YOU FOR CHRISTMAS

Father, we thank you for Christmas
and for the coming of Jesus Christ into this world.
Thank you that you have taught us to see and know you
through looking to him;
that he has shown us you are a God of love;
and that your love is real, strong, and very demanding.
We thank you that Jesus has shown us
that we need never be afraid
of the past, the future, or the present.
He has given us the assurance that because he is Immanuel,
he is always with us.

No matter who we are, no matter what we face,
he is Immanuel, always Immanuel;
God with us—always. **Amen.**

CHRIST—THE PROMISE OF HOPE

Lord, we thank you that, in the birth of your Son,
you have made the down payment on your promise
that you will always be with us.
In all the twists and turns of life—
you are there, always there.
You have promised in Jesus to share the whole of life with us
and we are thankful—so very thankful.
We thank you too, Father, for the help, care,
and strength we receive
from our families, our friends, and our fellow Christians.
When we are low, sad, or afraid,
your love, through them, enables us to come through
with hope and joy, and our eyes
even more firmly fixed on him.
Thank you for each time,
when in the midst of our troubles,
problems, difficulties, anxieties, or pain,
we have been made more aware of your love
and our need to trust you in everything;
for each and every opportunity you give us
to share the love and knowledge we have of you
with those who feel unloved, unwanted, and unnecessary.
We ask that through your love
we may be enabled to make that love real for others too.

Forgive our words of fear, our thoughts
and feelings of uncertainty;
forgive our anger, our bitterness, and our refusal to forgive.
Father, forgive us that so easily
we allow the things that crowd into our lives
to crowd you out.
Forgive us and make us new.
This we ask in Jesus' name. **Amen.**

HIGHLY FAVOURED

Lord, we are so highly favoured.
Your love met us at our births and has come with us
on the journey of our lives to this moment in time.
Your love goes before us, preparing the way,
and your love is with us from this day on.
So often the future appears dark, empty, and uncertain.
We do not know what tomorrow will bring
but we trust that through the darkest hour
your light will shine and that it will scatter the darkness;
that it will show the way through the most fearful day
until that time when we enter the light
of the knowledge of your love.
Father, we praise you for all that you have done
and all that you continue to do for us,
in and through Jesus Christ.
We thank you that he came
and we thank you more that he still comes.
Though there is often still no room, he goes on coming.
Lord, as we hear again the story of that first Christmas,

may we not close our inward ears
to what you are saying to us.
Tell us again of your power, your rejection of all that is evil,
and of the hope that nothing,
but nothing, that the world can say or do
can ever take away or spoil the wonder
of your love and peace.
Lord, give us again that peace that passes all understanding,
the peace that only Christ, the Prince of Peace, can give.
As we sing our carols, help us, we pray, to come to know
the Saviour and Lord to whom they point.
And in knowing him, may we begin to know that life
which is like experiencing Christmas every day.
Father, we have prepared many things this Christmas;
help us, we pray, to allow you to prepare our hearts and lives
to worship him who is Lord of all.
Through Christ our Lord. **Amen.**

CHRISTMAS DAY

Heavenly Father, we praise you for Jesus Christ
and for his coming among us at Christmas.
It is so easy to think that we don't count,
that we have been forgotten, or that no one cares.
We praise you that in your Son
we have one who assures us of your almighty presence
and proves that your love is truly
for each and every one of us.
Father, we praise you for Jesus Christ
and for the value he gives to our lives
as we live them in faith, hope, and love.

It is as we look to him that we know
some things are right and some things are wrong,
some things are against your will
and some things are within your purposes for our lives.
We thank you for all the fun and laughter,
for the joy and peace, and for time
with our families and friends.
We thank you too for the singing of carols
and for listening to the familiar Christmas story—
and that we can know that it is not just a story!
Help us not to lose our hold on Christ this Christmas.
Teach us again to remember
that the baby in the manger is the man on the cross
and the man on the cross is the Lord of the empty tomb
and the Lord of the empty tomb is the one
who is Lord of eternity.
We bring our prayer in the name of the King of Kings
and the Lord of Lords. **Amen.**

THE WORLD OF SNOW

Lord, we saw the snow, your snow.
It fell to the earth.
It was soft and gentle;
it was white, pure and white.
It covered the whole landscape—
trees, bushes, fields, hedgerows,
fences, roads, pavements, and houses.
Everywhere was covered with a layer of white.
It was pure and white, brilliantly white.
We were blinded, dazzled by its whiteness—it hurt our eyes.

Everywhere was pure and white and clean.

And then; and then we came.
We came with our cars and our buses, our lorries,
our bicycles, and our feet.
We churned up the pure white snow into a filthy black mess.

Your world, Lord, was once pure and clean—
just like the snow.
Everything that you had made was 'very good'.
And then; and then we came.
We came and we spoilt your world,
as we have spoilt our lives.
Your pure white world we have polluted
with our greed, pride, and selfishness.

And then; and then you came.
Immanuel, born in a manger in Bethlehem.
You came to make it possible for the world—
for our hearts and lives—
to be pure and white and clean again.

Lord, thank you for Christmas,
and that you have declared the love that never ends,
which can fill our lives and make all things new. **Amen.**

WE THINK WE ARE SO WISE

Lord, we think we are so wise,
but your greatness is beyond our comprehension.

We think we are good, but your holiness
is beyond our reach.
We seek to be loving people,
but your love is beyond anything we can understand.
We come, as the humble and wise
of every generation have come,
to worship you, to acknowledge that you are
and always will be beyond anything
our tiny, finite minds can comprehend.
Fill us with your Spirit, accept our praise,
and glorify your name in Christ our Lord. **Amen.**

WE COME

Lord, we come with our lives,
our thoughts, our hopes, and our fears.
We come with our plans, our dreams, and our memories.
We come with our time, our gifts, and our skills.
We come with our family, our friends,
and we come with ourselves.
We come to offer to you everything we have and are.
We come to glorify your holy name. **Amen.**

THE VISIT

Lord, we come again to this place where you are worshipped.
We come to gather up all
we have said and done and thought
since last we met and bring it as part
of our offering of thanks and praise.

We have come to seek your truth, to praise your glory,
and to allow the light of your love
to drive the darkness out of our lives. **Amen.**

YOUR PRESENCE

Lord, your presence lifts us, your grace amazes us,
your power overwhelms us, and your love excites us.
No matter what we bring with us—
hurts, sorrows, self-satisfaction, bitterness, or joyful praise—
you always receive us as we are,
transform what we bring,
and fill us with gifts of your mercy. **Amen.**

PRAYERS OF PRAISE

LIVING GOD

We praise you, the one true, living God,
who fills the whole universe with life, love, and meaning.
We praise you for your tremendous love
which flows to us and into our lives in Christ.

It was your love, like that of the prodigal son's father,
that meant you simply longed to welcome us home.
Jesus' birth in Bethlehem was a sign
of the depths of your love
and that he was born as a baby just as we are;
we now know there is nothing
that will make you stop loving us.

Lord, it is your love that takes the people we are
and makes it possible for us to be transformed
into the people we are meant to be.
We praise you for your love which sets us free
from everything that holds us,
from everything that squeezes real life out of us,
and brings us out of darkness
into the glorious light of the Father's presence.

We praise you for reaching out for us
and welcoming us home
and for making us your sons and daughters.
We praise you for the rest, refreshment, and hope
with which you promise to fill our lives.
We praise you for the assurance that we will share
in the joyful celebration of your creative love
and fill the universe with your glory.

Because of Jesus' birth in Bethlehem
we can know what it means to be loved by you
and through your life, death, and resurrection
we can have assurance of your touch of grace upon our days.

We praise you here, we praise you now,
we will praise you everywhere we go, as long as we live.
We will praise you eternally
in ever-increasing joy and worship,
with Jesus Christ our Lord. **Amen.**

ULTIMATE CONTROL

Father, we have come to praise you for who you are
and for what you have done for us.
We praise you for your glory, your authority,
your sovereignty,
and your ultimate control over all things.

We praise you for the life you have given us
and the freedom to choose what you have provided.

We praise you that though we have used our freedom
to turn our backs on you,
to please ourselves, and to go our own way,
your loving-kindness has always been there for us.
We praise you for loving us enough to hold us, heal us,
and welcome us home whenever we turn to you
for forgiveness and cleansing.
We praise you for all you have done for us
through Jesus Christ, your Son, our Lord.
We praise you for the way his parents brought him
to the temple as a helpless baby.
We praise you for the assurance that we too can come
in our weakness and emptiness
and know that you will accept and renew us.
We praise you for your victory of love
over our guilt and despair
and for the promise that we shall, by faith in him,
share in the heaven of your love.
We offer our praise to you now
and through all the days of our lives
until we praise in eternity
and give you glory in the name of Christ our Lord. **Amen.**

FOCUSED IN JESUS

Almighty God, our heavenly Father,
we praise you for being with us,
and for being with us in Christ.
Your almighty presence gives us such hope and strength.
All our praise is focused in Jesus.

We remember today his visit to the temple.
From before his birth through to his death on the cross
his purpose was not only to make you real for us
and your love known,
but to make it effective and active
in the lives of all your people.
His resurrection demonstrated the power
you are always making available for all your people.
We praise you that you are not a God
of our own imagination
nor are you absent, remote, unmoved, or unfeeling.
We worship you, the one true, living God,
who is very real, very near, and present and active
in the world that Christ died to heal.
We seek to praise you in the words we speak,
the songs we sing, and in the lives we live.
Lord, you are wiser than all our words,
more beautiful than all our songs,
and more loving than our lives will ever be.
We have come to celebrate your glory
and to declare that you are worthy of the worship
that streams to you from one end of time to the other.
Like your Son, we come to your house to worship you,
our Father and our God. **Amen.**

WE ADORE YOU!

Amazing God! We adore you and we praise you.
We bring our praises in the name of Jesus Christ,
your Son, our Lord.

He was born among us!
He was born one of us!
He was born one for us!
He was born to be with us!
He was born that we might live!
He was born that we might become children of God!

We praise you for the way he demonstrated your merciful love
and your gentle touch upon our lives.
We praise you for his coming as light for all your people
of every age and in every place.
We praise you for his coming to set us free,
to open blind eyes, and to heal broken hearts and lives.
We praise you for his readiness to enter into
all that life in this world means to us, that we might,
by your grace, share all that heaven is in him.
We praise you for the way he identified himself with us.
He entered into our pain, our rejection,
our sorrow, our hopes,
and through his baptism, he even tasted
the results and effects of our sinfulness.
We praise you for accepting his sacrifice on the cross
as the price of the healing of our relationship with you.
We praise you more that through his resurrection
he has guaranteed our share in his eternal kingdom.
Lord, our praises are limited by time and space
and by our human weakness.
By your grace, enable us and empower us
that we shall be with you and praise you for ever in
　　Christ. **Amen.**

PRAYERS OF THANKSGIVING

THE WISE MEN

Lord, we thank you for your coming to us in Jesus Christ
and that through him you have made yourself known.
You have spoken to us through him
in a way that we could hear and understand.
We thank you for his appearing
for all people of every age and every place;
for the way that your Spirit spoke to the wise men
all those years ago.
They represent all
who do not know you and are far from you.
They stand for those
who long for something of which they are only dimly aware.
We thank you for the way the Spirit compelled your church
to open its heart and mind and welcome all people,
Jew and Gentile, into its fellowship.
We praise you for the way that the good news
has been faithfully proclaimed all around the world;
for the immense variety of languages, customs,
and styles of worship

that are used by the worldwide church of Jesus Christ.
We thank you for every sign
of hope, peace, and reconciliation
made possible in and through your church;
for our place in your church
and for our communion with you and with one another.
We bring our thanks in the name of Christ the Lord. **Amen.**

INDISCRIMINATE LOVE

Father, we thank you for your indiscriminate love
that reaches out to each and every person.
We thank you for your love that will not be defeated
by our sinful world or by our selfish lives.
We thank you that your love is always reaching out,
seeking those who are lost, healing those who are broken,
and holding those who are hurting.
We thank you that you keep the door ever open
and rejoice whenever someone turns to you
in trust and hope.
Father, we thank you for those you have used
to touch and change our lives.
We thank you for those who, like the parents of Jesus,
brought us in faith to offer us to you.
We thank you that though we were not able
to understand our baptism,
it remains for us a true picture of grace.
We thank you that our baptism need not
and cannot be repeated;
help us to accept that we are accepted.

We thank you for preachers and Sunday school teachers,
for family and friends, and all who,
through their words and example,
made Christ real for us and nurtured our faith in him.
We thank you for the fellowship of Christians
and for worship each Sunday,
for reading your Word and for the joy of praying,
and for all opportunities you provide for us
to walk in your light and discover your glory.
May all we learn of Christ and everything we receive
through the Spirit
enable us to become channels of grace to our neighbour.
Amen.

SENSE OF GRATITUDE

Father, we thank you that we can come to you
in the knowledge that we are not only loved,
but that there is no one anywhere who has
or will love us more.
We come with a sense of gratitude that wells up within us
and overflows in thankfulness and joy.
We thank you that we can come as we are,
that we can come without fear,
that we can come without any need
to persuade you to love us.
We thank you that we can come
with no need to prove our worth
for we can come knowing that we are already accepted.
We thank you that we can come at all.

Father, we thank you that we can come to be set free
from everything that makes us like slaves
and from everything that fills us with fear.
We thank you for your offer to set us free
from all our negative attitudes,
from our broken promises,
and from all our good intentions that came to nothing.
Thank you for your liberating power
that is available to us anywhere and everywhere.
Thank you for setting us free from all that fills us
with a sense of guilt
and from those things that make us ashamed.
Thank you for the promise of ever-increasing joy
as we respond with love to your love,
in the knowledge that we are your children,
not by right but by grace alone.
We bring our thanks in the name of our brother,
Jesus Christ. **Amen.**

WHEN WE WERE HURTING

Father, we thank you for those who stood by us
when we were hurting and loved us
even when we were in the wrong.
We thank you for men and women
who share the plight of those less fortunate than themselves,
those who work for the good of their neighbour,
those who go the extra mile and turn the other cheek.
We thank you for those who do all they can
to make others feel comfortable, accepted, and valued.

We thank you for those who make no pretence
of greatness or superiority
but stand alongside their neighbour—
no matter what the cost.
Thank you for those whose gracious words and caring deeds
enable others to have self-respect and hope.
Thank you for every opportunity to love our neighbour
and be representatives of your almighty, humble, holy love.
In the name of Christ our Lord. **Amen.**

PRAYERS OF CONFESSION

NARROW-MINDEDNESS

Father, forgive our narrow-mindedness and our prejudice
for accepting only that which we can understand
and those with whom we agree.
Forgive our too easy rejection of other people
and their styles of worship, their hopes, and their fears.
Forgive our unwillingness to be enriched
by one another's insights, one another's prayers,
and one another's praise.
Forgive and warm our cold hearts,
awaken our closed minds,
invigorate our tired praise.
Set our lives ablaze with your love
so that we may love, serve, and hear you all the time
and everywhere so that you may receive
the glory you deserve. **Amen.**

HALF-HEARTED COMMITMENT

Father, forgive us our half-hearted commitment,
the poverty of our worship,
and the frailty of our faith in Christ.
Forgive us our lack of prayer
and our failure to bring family and friends,
our colleagues at work,
and those who live near us to the feet of Christ.
Forgive our lack of hope and trust.
Forgive our lack of discipline
and that we need to return to you
to confess the same mistakes again and again.
Forgive us our failure to live in the knowledge
that the good news is really true.
Forgive us that we live as if Christ had never been born,
never lived, never died,
or as if he is still in the tomb.
Forgive us that we refuse to be channels to others
of the love, mercy, and grace that we have received.
Forgive us for every person who,
because of our weak faith and the poverty of our witness,
is living less richly than they should.
Forgive us our timidity and our self-centredness
and make us ambassadors for Christ. **Amen.**

NEVER SATISFIED

Father, forgive us for being the kind of people we are.
We are never satisfied, never content with what we have.
So we are ever anxious, often angry,
sometimes envious and jealous.
We are concerned for our own needs
but careless of one another's.
We allow ourselves to descend
to the level of the rest of creation
and the survival of the fittest.
Open our lives again to your fatherly love.
Hold us, forgive us, and transform us.
Give us in all of life's pain and sorrow
peace and joy in Christ our Lord. **Amen.**

PRAYERS FOR ALL AGES

GIFTS AND SKILLS

Father, we praise you for the gifts and skills
that you have put into our lives,
and that we have eyes to see, ears to hear, and minds to think.
We praise you for putting within each of us
a longing to know more and more about your world
and about all the things we see.
We thank you for all those who have used
their time and their talents
to discover so many important things
and to make life easier and safer for many people;
for all those good things that human beings have made
and that have added so much to our daily lives.
We thank you for televisions and heart monitors,
for washing machines and spacecraft,
for motor cars, aeroplanes, and computers,
for electronic games and mobile phones.

We praise you for lives saved and for the fun and excitement
many inventions have added to our lives

and for making us want to know more and more.
We thank you for Jesus, your greatest gift of all.
It is only when we know him as Saviour and Lord
that we will be able to use our minds and our ideas
and all the things that we have made
for your praise and glory.
Forgive us whenever we put our possessions before people
and ourselves and our dreams before the needs of others.
Forgive us whenever we put anyone or anything before you.
Forgive us for pleasing ourselves
and not listening to your call to love our neighbour as ourselves.
Hear our prayer and fill us again
with your love and joy. **Amen.**

YOU HAVE MADE US

Father, we thank you for the way you have made us
so that we can think, plan, choose, and give,
and that we can help, care, and share with one another.
We praise you that you not only made us
but that you made us to share
in friendship and fellowship with one another.
We praise you for those who love us and care for us
and care about us
and for those who are special people in our lives.
We are sorry that so many people feel alone and unwanted
and are treated as if they are simply numbers.
We thank you that you have never thought of us like that.
You made us so that we can enjoy being
in one another's company

and can share love and happiness, joy and pleasure,
kindness and peace.
We remember that Jesus was brought as a tiny baby
to your temple in Jerusalem.
It was his parents' way of reminding themselves
and those around them that our lives are a gift from you
and that all life belongs to you.
We thank you that whether we are single or married,
on our own or part of a group,
we can still enjoy the feeling of belonging
to our family and friends,
those with whom we work, and those we meet at school.
We thank you most of all that through Jesus
we can know that we belong to you and your family.
We ask that what we say and do and how we live
will make others want to belong to the family of God too.
In the name of Jesus, our brother and our friend. **Amen.**

WE HAVE COME

Lord, we have come to sing our hymns and our songs,
to say our prayers, and to hear your word in the Bible.
We do this so that we may hear the things
you want to say to us
about our lives and about our world
and so that we may be able to put you
at the centre of everything.
Lord, it is not easy to keep our eyes fixed on Jesus;
each day we find that there are so many other things
that we are tempted to put in his place

and there are so many other people
who want us to put them first instead of him.
We praise you for Jesus and for his love
for each and every one of us.
We thank you that he always puts us
at the very centre of his care
and he is always seeking the very best for us.
We know that he promised that those
who do put him and his love at the centre of their lives,
he will give them life that is real.
We thank you for the way he shows us that he wants
our lives to be free from everything that would spoil them
and from everything that would make us feel like prisoners.
We praise you that through his life, death, and resurrection
you have done everything to set us free
from the things that make us afraid, worried, and uncertain.
We thank you for your promise
that you will go on working in our hearts and lives
to make us the people you always meant us to be.
We ask your forgiveness for the way we make life hard
for other people
and for those times when we want our own way.
Forgive us and set us free and fill us with your love.
In Jesus' name. **Amen.**

YOUR WORLD

Heavenly Father, we thank you for the world
in which we live.
We thank you for its beauty;

for the different colours, shapes, and sizes
of everything around us.
We thank you for our family and friends,
for our neighbours, and those we spend our time with
at school and at work.
We thank you for making us, and for making us
the way we are.
Thank you that we can think and plan and choose and learn.
Thank you that we can help and care
and that we can give and receive.
Thank you that you have made us
so that we can laugh and we can cry;
we can work and we can play; we can toil and we can rest.
Thank you that you love us
and that we can love other people and they can love us.
Thank you most of all for Jesus; through him
you have shown us
just how much you love us and how much
you want to change our lives.
Through Jesus you have made it possible for us
to know you as our heavenly Father
and to know what it means to belong to your worldwide family.
Forgive us that we find it so easy
to receive gifts of love, help, and care
but that we are only willing to offer them
to those who are kind to us.
Forgive us most of all where we are unforgiving
and make us new and clean again.
We ask our prayer in the name of Jesus Christ,
the friend of those who get their lives into a mess. **Amen.**

PRAYERS FOR INTERCESSIONS

WISDOM

Lord, we pray for wisdom for parents;
for those bringing children up alone or in a family;
for those under pressure or strain;
and for parents uncertain of employment
and how to keep themselves out of debt;
for those concerned for their children's welfare and future.
May the light of Christ be the source of wisdom for all parents.
In the name of Jesus,
we ask our prayer.

Lord, we pray for wisdom for all politicians;
for those who came into politics with high ideals
and a genuine desire to seek justice and truth;
for those whose values and judgements are shaped
by their knowledge of the Scriptures and their love of the Lord.
We pray that the light of Christ
may be the source of wisdom for all politicians.
In the name of Jesus,
we ask our prayer.

Lord, we pray for wisdom for our world.
We pray for those who struggle for justice
for the deprived and despairing;
for those who are seeking
to make the world a cleaner, safer, and fairer place for all;
for industrial leaders who give no thought
for the impact on future generations
of profit-driven choices that are being made today.
May the light of Christ be the source of wisdom
for all the world.
In the name of Jesus,
we ask our prayer.

Lord, we pray for wisdom for people;
for those trapped by the offer of instant solutions
to their problems for today,
but who have no answer to the debts
that must be faced tomorrow;
for those enslaved by the false security offered by lotteries;
and for those who ignore the fact that sudden riches
for some must be paid for by those who can least afford it.
We pray for those seeking to be faithful to Christ
and the gospel of love
in a world that has turned its back on its Maker.
In the name of Jesus,
we ask our prayer.

Lord, we pray for wisdom for all young people;
for those seeking guidance for their future studies
and those still seeking employment in their chosen profession;

for young people finding it all but impossible just to say no
in the face of pressure from their peers;
and for those who have made Christ Lord of their hearts.
May he also be Lord of their plans and dreams,
their choices and all their relationships.
May the light of Christ be their source of wisdom.
In the name of Jesus,
we ask our prayer.

We pray for wisdom for ourselves.
May the light of Christ be the source of our wisdom.
In all that we face and in all that we choose;
in all we plan and everything we desire;
in all our relationships and in all our service;
in all our commitments and all our obedience;
in all our pain and in all our pleasure;
in all our successes and in all our failures;
in all our joys and in all our sorrows;
in all our walking with God and trusting in Jesus;
in all our waiting on the Spirit and in all our surrender.
In the name of Jesus,
we ask our prayer. Amen.

THINK OF SOMEONE

Think of someone who feels that their life is empty,
someone who is overwhelmed by a sense
of their own unworthiness,
someone who has been made to feel useless
and now finds it hard to live life to the full.

May the presence of Christ and the power of the Spirit
    transform their lives.

Think of someone who is hurting,
someone who is facing a time of bereavement or loss,
someone who is facing the loss of employment,
which has been the source of security
and given them a purpose in life,
someone who is needing to learn that they still matter
even when the family has left home.
May the presence of Christ and the power of the Spirit give
    them hope.

Think of someone who is facing a time of illness or pain,
someone who has taken good health for granted
and now is finding it hard to accept their new situation,
someone trying to come to terms with a terminal illness
and for those who are longing to give them the love
and support they will need.
May the presence of Christ and the power of the Spirit hold
    them and make them whole.

Think of our worship and how it might be more worthy,
more relevant, and more challenging.
Think of our service to the local community
and think of our witness to Jesus as Lord.
Think of all who offer their time, their talents,
and themselves
in the service of Christ's church.
May the presence of Christ and the power of the Spirit

be the source of our strength and the reason for service.

Think of the other churches in this area
and of ways we might worship, witness,
and serve God together.
Think of their leaders and their congregations.
Think of all that we share in common.
Think of how our differences look to a lost world
and in the context of heaven.
May the presence of Christ and the power of the Spirit open
   our hearts to one another.

Think of any you know to be in any particular need.
Think of yourself and all that concerns you.
Think of all that you must face in the coming days of this week.
Think of your worries, your fears, and your need
of knowing that you matter.
May the presence of Christ and the power of the Spirit hold
   you still.

Lord, in your mercy, **hear our prayer.**

In Christ's name. **Amen.**

MAKE US WHAT YOU MEANT US TO BE

Father, we come in Christ to pray for the church
and the world.
We pray for all Christians everywhere
that they may come to you

in the sure and simple way that Christ
came to his Father's house.
Be there, we pray,
for those who seek you with heart and soul
and mind and strength,
and be with those who go in your name
to love their neighbours as themselves.
Lord, by your grace,
make us what you meant us to be.

Lord, make us your witnesses.
So fill our lives with your love and your truth
that others will know we have been with Christ.
Many of those we meet are living small,
cramped, empty lives;
they are existing when you intended them to live;
they are hanging on by the skin of their teeth
when you are offering life in all its fullness.
We pray that what we say and how we say it,
what we do and how we do it
will enable those who do not know you
to be caught up by the wonder of your love for them.
Lord, by your grace,
make us what you meant us to be.

Lord, make us your servants.
So touch our lives by your Holy Spirit
that we may be equipped
to care for the careless, love the unlovable,
and enable the ungrateful to give thanks.

Lord, call us to be your servants
to those whom life treats harshly,
those overwhelmed by grief and loss,
those who are finding life hard to cope with,
those who are crushed or defeated
by the demands and expectations of others or themselves;
for those who are poor, hungry, homeless,
or lacking the skills necessary to live in our modern world.
Lord, by your grace,
make us what you meant us to be.

Lord, make us your channels of hope
and healing and wholeness
to those who are broken and defeated by life.
We remember those we know to be in need
of your healing touch.
We think of those who are ill,
those who are lonely or afraid,
those who are dying,
and those who watch with them;
those filled with regrets or remorse,
those who do not know which way to turn,
those for whom the bottom has dropped out of their lives.
We pray that the light of your mercy may reach
into the darkest corners of life.
Lord, by your grace,
make us what you meant us to be.

Lord, we pray for ourselves.
Keep our eyes fixed on Christ, the source of all faith,

hope, and love.
In him bring our faith to perfection
that by your Holy Spirit it may come to full bloom
as we feel your touch in every part of our lives.
In the stillness, we open our lives to you and your will.
By your Spirit, may our lives honour you
and our dying glorify you
with praise that never ends for all eternity.
Lord, by your grace,
make us what you meant us to be.

In the name of Christ. **Amen.**

THE WORLD

Father, we pray for your world.
As Christ stood alongside us in all our sinfulness
and the poverty of our lives,
enable us to stand with all those who are facing
the brunt of human wickedness.
We pray, Lord, that as you send us out
you will fill us with all the love and tenderness of Christ.
Send us to love the helpless, hold the broken,
and risk our own peace for the sake of others.
Lord, transform the words of our prayers
into lives lived for your glory.

Lord, we pray for all people and all nations
whose intentions for good
are undermined by the emptiness and foolishness

of those around them.
We pray for those whose lives are being spoilt
by the selfishness and self-centredness of others.
We pray for those whose hopes and joys
are being eroded by the lack of responsibility of others.
Give us the love and compassion to stand with those
who stand alone.
Lord, transform the words of our prayers
into lives lived for your glory.

Lord, we pray for those who are robbed of their innocence;
for children who are physically and sexually abused
or exploited;
for those who are treated differently
because of their colour, nationality, gender, ability,
or disability.
Give us the determination to share the love of Christ
which knows no boundaries and accepts no barriers
or limitations.
Lord, transform the words of our prayers
into lives lived for your glory.

Lord, we pray for all who are being made slaves to drugs
and those who are being drawn into petty crime
to pay for their habit.
We pray for those who have stepped over the threshold
into ruthless crime which causes others fear and insecurity.
We pray for those who confuse self-centred ambition
and greed
with personal freedom and personal choice.

May our lives in Christ go on being salt for the world.
Lord, transform the words of our prayers
into lives lived for your glory.

Lord, we pray for the elderly;
those so often and so easily terrified by violence
and who are neglected by a fast-changing world.
We pray for all who feel isolated and vulnerable
in a society designed for the young, the fit, and the active.
We pray for communities that have lost sight
of your love and compassion.
Enable us, we pray, to be channels of Christ's love
as we share in the hurt of our neighbours.
Lord, transform the words of our prayers
into lives lived for your glory.

Lord, we pray for all who are confused by the pain
and suffering in your world.
We pray that all Christians may demonstrate
in the way they live and speak and by their care
and understanding
that the God of love is still present and active in his world
and he is entering fully into its pain and distress.
Give us, Lord, the ability to begin where people are and,
by your grace, lead them gently closer to you.
Lord, transform the words of our prayers
into lives lived for your glory.

Lord, we pray for ourselves.
Teach us new words to say, new things to do,

and new lives to live
that we may, by the power of your Spirit,
be ever more open to your life-changing,
world-transforming grace.
Help us to realise all over again our uniqueness in your sight.
Teach us once more that our value is measured
only by the empty cross and the empty tomb.
Lord, transform the words of our prayers
into lives lived for your glory.

Hear our prayers in the name of Christ,
the one who walked where we walk
and shared all that life means to us. **Amen.**

PRAYERS OF COMMITMENT

CALL US TO FOLLOW

Come, Lord Jesus, call us to follow you
and inspire us to serve you.
Challenge us to care for one another
and enable us to demonstrate your love
as you fill us with your grace. **Amen.**

WE BRING

Lord,
we bring you our unbelief that you may give us faith;
we bring you our self-reliance that we may learn to trust;
we bring you our self-satisfaction that we might be changed;
we bring you our weakness so that we can be made strong;
we bring you our emptiness in order to be filled;
we bring you our trust that we might be sent;
we bring you our love that you might commission us to serve;
we bring you our lives and make our commitment.
We ask for your presence and to be filled with your Spirit.
Amen.

WHERE THERE IS A CROSS

Father,
when there is a cross, we will carry it;
when we pass through despair, we will endure it;
when our peace is broken, we will suffer it;
when we mourn, we will do it bravely;
when we are overwhelmed, we will do so
trusting in your promises alone.
Whatever we face, whatever happens, wherever we go,
keep us true to you, filled with Christ,
and overflowing with the Spirit. **Amen.**

IDENTIFIED

As Christ identified himself with those whose lives
were in a mess
and who were far from God, and as he gave his life for all,
help us, weak and imperfect as we are,
to follow his example as we walk in the steps
and rely on the power of Jesus. **Amen.**

PRAYERS FOR DISMISSAL

GO NOW

Go now in the joy of Christ,
the power of the Spirit,
and in the love of God. **Amen.**

SEND US OUT

Lord, send us out in your name
to serve the world and to love our neighbour as ourselves.
Send us out in faith and hope
that we may be channels of your grace to all. **Amen.**

WE HAVE BEGUN

We have begun an act of praise and adoration
that will never end;
we have drawn closer to the God who will never leave us;
we have opened our hearts to the Spirit
who will hold us for ever. **Amen.**

WHEREVER YOU GO

Wherever you go, claim the presence of Christ;
whoever you are confronting, remember
Christ died for them too;
whatever you are facing, remember
that you do so in the power
that raised Christ from the dead. **Amen.**

ABOUT THE AUTHOR

David Clowes, born in Ellesmere Port, left school at fifteen following a secondary modern education. In 1965 he committed his life to Christ at Heaton Mersey Methodist and in 1967 he received God's call into the Methodist ministry. He trained at Hartley Victoria College and gained a degree in theology at Manchester University.

David served in a number of churches in the northwest of England before retiring in 2010 after thirty-five years in active ministry. His first book, *500 Prayers for All Occasions*, began as a spiritual exercise during a sabbatical. This was followed by *500 More Prayers for All Occasions*. His third book of prayers, *500 Prayers for the Christian Year*, is based on scriptures from the Revised Common Lectionary.

David is married to Angela, and they have two married sons, a foster son, and four grandchildren.